Grass Tree, Flinders Ranges National Park, South Australia.

STEVE PARISH

DISCOVER
AUSTRALIA

PHOTOGRAPHY STEVE PARISH

TEXT PAT SLATER

Steve Parish
PUBLISHING

Steve Parish Publishing Pty Ltd
www.steveparish.com.au

Cape York Peninsula, like so much of Australia, offers the traveller new worlds of adventure and discovery.

INTRODUCTION

Memories shape our lives.

Memories remind us of our successes and our failures, allow us to daydream and to drift in time. In memories, we can revisit the beautiful places of our world, relive experiences which made us what we are today.

Our human senses are often the magical passwords that open the doors into the world of memory. For me, the sense of sight is extremely powerful. When I remember a scene, my mind produces immediate mental images of forms, shapes, colours and textures.

Because of this strong visual imaging ability and a love for the natural world, I took up photography at an early age and for many years concentrated my efforts on wildlife and wild places. Finally, because I wanted to produce images which included all of Australia, I had to venture into the cities. My first experiences at urban street photography were quite painful - the noise and bustle and crowds of people were, to me, a waking nightmare.

Gradually I adapted and learned to appreciate the forms, shapes, colours and textures of the cities and towns of Australia. Now, after some years of "street-walking" with my cameras, I feel I am discovering my country all over again, as a nation of people living and growing together.

In this book, I have gathered together photographs which for me epitomise Australia. I have included the continent's major natural areas and some of the wild creatures which live there. I have added images of Australia's built environment and momentary encounters with the people of Australia at work and at play.

As you turn the pages of this book, I hope you will share my ongoing discovery of this wonderful country.

Steve Parish

AUSTRALIA'S NATIONAL CAPITAL

It is a delight to go sightseeing in Canberra. The city has something to offer everyone, with its magnificent lake, its wonderful gardens, its impressive national buildings and monuments, its embassies, excellent shops and great restaurants.

It is easy to find Canberra's landmarks. Walter Burley Griffin's plan for Canberra, finally implemented in 1925, visualised a Parliamentary Triangle which would join places on a land axis running from Mount Ainslie through Red Hill to Bimberi Peak with those on a water axis and a municipal axis. Seven decades of civic achievement since then have developed the city as a worthy National Capital.

Canberra is a year-round mecca for visitors. Autumn brings spectacular foliage to parks and gardens. Summer is excellent for exploring the cool interiors of institutions such as Parliament House and the National Gallery. Winter means crisp cold, perhaps snow and a local passion for Rugby League. Spring sees Floriade, the festival of flowers and a chance to experience this very contemporary city in party mood.

Within the limits of the Australian Capital Territory are Tidbinbilla Nature Reserve, with its famous mob of kangaroos and other wildlife, Cockington Green's miniature village, Mt Stromlo Observatory - these and other attractions are well worth a visit.

Below: The Carillon on Aspen Island, in Canberra's Lake Burley Griffin, was a 1963 gift from the British Government.
Opposite: A view of Canberra from Mount Ainslie shows a green, tree-filled city on the shores of a placid lake.
Following pages: Walter Burley Griffin's land axis is focused on Capital Hill and the Houses of Parliament,
then crossed by the water axis formed by Lake Burley Griffin. On the further shore of the lake,
Anzac Parade leads to the Australian War Memorial, at the foot of Mount Ainslie.

Parliament House: Seat of Australian government

The original Parliament House was erected in 1927. Today, the old building has been superseded by the new Parliament House opened by Queen Elizabeth II on 9th May, 1988. The summit of Capital Hill was excavated, then assembled again around the new construction, so that today Parliament House appears part of the landscape, retaining the grand vista of Walter Burley Griffin's vision. New Parliament House contains more than 2,000 rooms, which are open to the public 364 days of the year. A fine view of Canberra can be seen from the walkway that passes over the building.

★

Above: This transitional Parliament House was opened in 1927 and served until 1988.
Below: Australia's Coat of Arms is a familiar motif in Canberra.
Opposite: Michael Nelson Tjakamarra designed the mosaic before Parliament House, which symbolises the coming-together of Dreamtime ancestors to enact ceremonial "business".

Canberra: Showplace for Nature's beauty

All land in Canberra is owned by the Federal Government and development here has been controlled carefully. This is a city which favours trees over billboards, and lawns and gardens over concrete and paving. Those who love open spaces and green places feel at home here.

The starkness of Canberra's winter, when many deciduous trees are leafless, is followed by a blaze of spring blooms. Commonwealth Park, with its lovely annual display of tulips, is only one of many lakeside recreational areas, while in the Australian National Botanic Gardens, on the lower slopes of Black Mountain, are to be found plants native to this country displayed in regional groupings.

Above: October blossom frames the Terrestrial Globe on Regatta Point and, in the distance, the Australian National Library.
Opposite: Each Springtime, Floriade sees Commonwealth Park ablaze with flowers.

Canberra: An overview of an elegant city

During the Canberra Festival each March, a fleet of hot-air balloons takes those eager to see Canberra from the air on a never-to-be-forgotten journey. Looking down upon this largest of Australia's inland cities, the impression is of elegant proportions, impressive public buildings and sparkling water, circled with parklands and enhanced by neat, well-planned suburbs.

★

Above: In March each year, the Canberra Festival sees balloons drift buoyantly in front of Parliament House.

Canberra: A city for outdoor pleasures

Canberra's parks are designed so people using them can walk, cycle, picnic or just sit, appreciating the harmony of water, sky and trees. The contrast between exotic plant species and Australian natives adds to the variety of the landscape. Autumn in this inland city is cold enough to colour deciduous leaves and Canberra's gardens are magnificent in this mellow, fruitful season.

✸

Above: April brings warm tones to Canberra's deciduous trees.

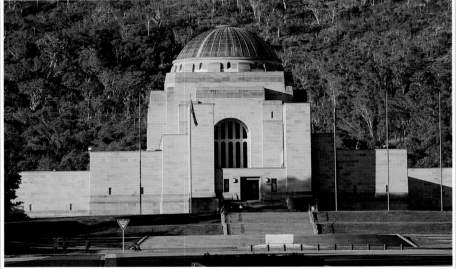

The Australian War Memorial: Lest We Forget

The Australian War Memorial is for many people one of Canberra's major attractions. It is a shrine which honours over 100,000 Australians who gave their lives in times of war. The National Anzac Day ceremony is held here each 25th April.

✦

Above: The Memorial's Pool of Reflection leads to the domed Hall of Memory.
Below: The Australian War Memorial.

The Australian War Memorial: "In Memoriam"

The many displays in the War Memorial provide insight into how Australians have played their parts once their country has been committed to conflict. Here are remembered men and women who were tested in time of war and not found wanting.

★

Above: An aerial view of the War Memorial complex.
Below: Stained-glass windows in the Hall of Memory.

National Gallery and High Court: Arts and Law

The magnificent National Gallery of Australia houses works from national and international collections in its eleven principal galleries on three levels. The High Court of Australia, opened in 1980, is the country's final court of appeal. Both institutions stand on the southern shore of Lake Burley Griffin.

★

Above: The High Court of Australia.
Below: The National Gallery of Australia.

The National Science and Technology Centre

At the National Science and Technology Centre in Canberra's King Edward Terrace, visitors can find out for themselves why things work and apply scientific principles to a variety of activities. The Centre, a joint Australian and Japanese Bicentennial project, was opened in November, 1988.

★

Above: The National Science and Technology Centre of Australia.

NEW SOUTH WALES

THE PREMIER STATE

The State of New South Wales was established in 1788, when Captain Arthur Phillip founded a British penal colony at Sydney Cove. In the two centuries since, New South Wales, which occupies around ten per cent of Australia's mainland, has become a major primary and industrial producer, containing over one-third of the continent's population, most of them living along the fertile coastal strip.

No discovery of Australia would be complete without experiencing Sydney, a cosmopolitan city where whatever a visitor seeks can be found. Sydney offers Port Jackson, the world's greatest harbour, a taste of history, cultural experiences, sophisticated pleasures or the simple life of sun and sea. It has the self-assurance of one of the world's great cities.

Behind the sun-blessed, fertile coast of New South Wales lies the Great Dividing Range, its slopes covered with lush rainforests in the northern parts of the State and rising to scenic alpine peaks towards the Victorian border.

Inland, over the range, are the grain-growing Western Plains, which shade into "the Outback". This is pastoral and mining country, a tough land, to be explored and savoured at leisure for its beauty, its wildlife and the unique characters of its hospitable people.

✦

Below: A replica of Captain Bligh's famous "Bounty" lies moored at Circular Quay, Sydney Cove.
Opposite: Sydney Opera House was lit in Olympic colours for the announcement that
Sydney will host the Olympic Games in the year 2000 (photo by Phillip Hayson).
Following pages: As night falls, Opera House and Harbour Bridge are illuminated above the wine-dark waters of Port Jackson.

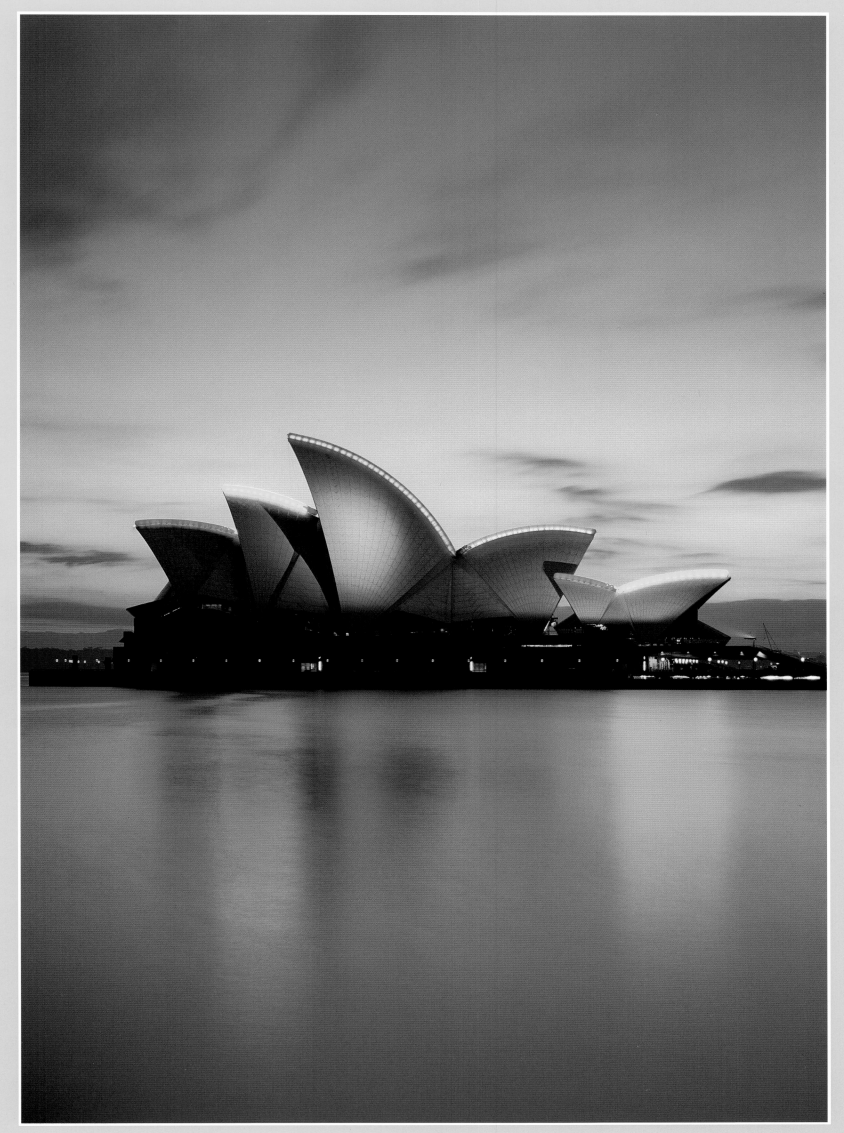

Darling Harbour: Harbourside hospitality

Darling Harbour was opened in 1988, after its renovation from a decrepit dockyard and railway goods terminal. It is now one of Sydney's major attractions, containing the Harbourside Festival Marketplace, the Sydney Aquarium, comprehensive convention centres, fine accommodation, promenades and the famous Chinese Garden.

This magnificent complex is reached by a walkway over the Pyrmont Bridge, or by a Sydney-scanning monorail, or by ferry. The weight gained by diners at the Darling Harbour restaurants can be walked off at the Sydney Aquarium, the Powerhouse Museum and the National Maritime Museum.

✴

Above: View towards Sydney city centre across the Darling Harbour complex.
Opposite: Twilight on the Harbourside Festival Marketplace and Novotel Hotel, Darling Harbour.
Previous pages: Sailing is a passion with Sydneysiders, who have the waters of Port Jackson at their disposal.

Old Sydney: History on display

If you want to savour the history of Sydney, go to The Rocks, where the site of early settlement grew into a nineteenth-century slum, which by the 1960s was seen as ready for demolition. The Rocks was saved and restored, and now provides a window into Sydney's past. Another rewarding expedition is to the Queen Victoria Building, symbol of Sydney's nineteenth-century prosperity from wool, wheat and gold. Once markets, it has been refurbished for modern times. The nearby Town Hall was completed in 1874.

★

Above: Queen Victoria in bronze sits outside the Queen Victoria Building and below the clock-tower of Sydney Town Hall.
Below: The historic Rocks area offers fascinating buildings from Sydney's convict and colonial days.
Opposite: The massive Queen Victoria Building, with its sandstone and stained glass, is now a venue for quality shops.
Following pages: The Three Sisters, in the Blue Mountains National Park, a scenic area which is close to Sydney.

The Blue Mountains: Beyond the blue horizon

The Blue Mountains, 65 kilometres from Sydney, have for more than a century provided a haven for people retreating from the city's bustle. Now the mountains' spectacular scenery and the opportunities they hold for adventure draw visitors from all over Australia and from abroad.

Rising to around 1,100 metres above sea-level, the mountains offer precipitous cliffs, deep forested gorges and bushwalking which will test even the experienced hiker. For the less energetic, there are scenic bus-tours, valley-viewing from the Katoomba Scenic Skyway and leisurely exploration of some of Australia's most beautiful gardens.

Blue Mountains National Park, gazetted in 1967, is around 240,000 hectares in extent. A noted scenic attraction, the Three Sisters are massive sandstone pillars which, according to legend, were once Aboriginal girls who were turned to stone by their father when they were threatened by a monster.

Above: The Waratah, floral emblem of New South Wales, bears brilliant, bird-attracting flowers in Spring.
Opposite: The Crimson Rosella is a colourful parrot, which is particularly common around Echo Point Lookout, from which the Three Sisters can be viewed.

Just playing in the sand

Australians love going to the beach. All ages, all shapes and sizes of human beings are to be found on Australia's beaches, soaking up the sun or shaded from its rays, swimming, surfing, playing games, sailing or just lying around, relaxing.

Not only pleasure-seekers throng to the beach. There are people who are serious about catching fish, there are divers, fitness fanatics and that archetypal Australian figure, the surf lifesaver, dedicated to keeping the unwary or unwise from a watery fate.

Sydney's northern beaches stretch from Manly, serviced by a ferry service dating back to 1847, to Palm Beach. To the south, Bondi (seven kilometres from the city), Coogee and Cronulla are popular.

The coast of New South Wales north and south of Sydney has some of the world's best beaches, with clear, sparkling water and free access to sand and ocean for all who enjoy relaxing at the seaside. The towns spaced along the coast are happy, welcoming places from which to explore these sunny shores.

Above: This popular beach is at Terrigal, on the Central Coast of NSW.
Above right: Bondi Beach, south of Port Jackson's South Head.
Centre right: Lifesavers keep Australian beaches safe.
Below right: Manly, one of Sydney's northern beaches, was named after Aborigines who were described as "manly" by Captain Arthur Phillip.

Byron Bay: An idyllic place

Byron Bay makes a great base from which to explore not only the beaches of the Northern Coast but also a hinterland of mountains and forests. The area has a long history as a meeting-place for social activities - Aboriginal people gathered here for thousands of years to enact ceremonies.

The magnificent forests of the area were logged in the second half of the nineteenth century and the timber sent cascading down gully "shoots" to be shipped from the town which was officially known as Byron Bay from 1884. Today, Byron Bay is a delightful town frequented by people who love the sea and all it has to offer and who enjoy the mild, subtropical climate, which allows rainforest to linger in areas such as the Booyong Nature Reserve.

✸

Above: Cape Byron is the most easterly point on the Australian mainland. Captain Cook named it in 1770, after the grandfather of the famous English poet Lord Byron.
Opposite: The lighthouse on Cape Byron was constructed in 1901. The rays of the lamp can be seen for 43 kilometres out to sea.

The Snowy Mountains: Year-round playground

The Snowy Mountains amply reward visitors at any season of the year. Winter sees the peaks covered with snow and the slopes with skiers. Spring melts the snow and brings wombats and wildflowers out to enjoy the sunshine. Summer attracts bushwalkers and anglers to enjoy the cool crisp air and magnificent scenery of the High Country.

★

*Above: The moon rises over the snow-clad Australian Alps,
summit of the Great Dividing Range.*
*Above right: Once almost inaccessible "high country" used in summer to pasture
sheep and cattle, the Alps have become a tourist and snow-sports mecca.*

Take a break on the road

Country towns once had four essential elements - the store, the pub, the school and the police station. Today, the teachers and police may have been moved to larger centres, but the store and the pub remain and there are always plenty of travellers to refresh themselves at these oases. Often, a picturesque, old-fashioned shop-front will hide very modern facilities.

★

Above and below: In the tiny town of Silverton these stores still proudly serve the public.
Silverton, near Broken Hill, NSW, has served as location for some noted movies set in the Australian Outback.

The faces tell it all

The character of the country creates the country character.
Hard work and the challenges of a tough environment have left
their legacy in these faces. The Outback has a powerful hold on
those who live there. If you are passing through, it is
worthwhile stopping off, yarning awhile and finding out just
what ties such remarkable people to this challenging country.

———————————————★———————————————

Top left and clockwise: Six faces of Australia's Outback: farmer, southern NSW;
cameleer and camel, western NSW; miner, Broken Hill; jillaroo, Western Plains; opal miner, Lightning Ridge.

VICTORIA

THE GARDEN STATE

One of the many beauties of Victoria is that, because of the great variety of landscape types within its boundaries, new vistas appear at almost every turn of the road. In a comparatively short journey, the traveller can experience mountains, lakes, pastures, forests, farmlands, arid country and spectacular coastal scenery. If you are that traveller, take time to discover the glorious Grampians, with their peaks, forests and heaths. Travel through the rich grazing-land of the Western District, then cruise along the Great Ocean Road, with pauses to marvel at Port Campbell National Park, or wander the rainforest gullies of the Otway Ranges. Visit the Alps, then take a trip down the majestic Murray River, life-support for south-eastern Australia.

At last, all roads come to Melbourne, a kaleidoscope of a city, glorious with its tree-bordered boulevards, fiercely competitive in its sporting life. This is a city whose inhabitants love to eat out and socialise along the banks of the Yarra, or on the Port Phillip beaches. It is at the same time a wonderful example of a nineteenth-century Victorian city and as contemporary as tomorrow.

Melbourne is a city with attitude, style and savvy. Its electric trams rock softly past ultra-modern shopping complexes and historic buildings, galleries and theatres, gardens and parklands. Near Melbourne, there are the Dandenong Ranges and the Mornington Peninsula, then the traveller can go on eastwards to lush Gippsland and the Lakes.

Below left to right: Captain Cook's Cottage stands in Fitzroy Gardens; Springtime's abundance is displayed in the Conservatory, Fitzroy Gardens; the Yarra River runs through the heart of Melbourne.
Opposite: Aerial view over the War Memorial to Melbourne city. In the centre, to the left of St Kilda Road, are the National Gallery of Victoria and the Victorian Arts Centre.

Flinders Street Station: Where journeys begin

It is said that if you stand near the main entrance to Flinders Street Station, sooner or later everyone you have ever known in Australia will pass by. The station was constructed in 1910, where Flinders Street crosses Swanston Street, and has been a hub of Victoria's magnificent railway system ever since. Standing opposite the Station are two very different Melbourne icons - St Paul's Cathedral and Young and Jacksons Hotel.

★

Above: Flinders Street Station shines brightly at night.
Above right: "Under the clocks" at Flinders Street Station is a popular meeting place for the people of Melbourne.
Following pages: left: The Yarra and Melbourne at dawn; right: footbridge from South Gate complex to the northern bank of the Yarra River.

Above left: Balloon and biplane in front of the historic Shot Tower inside the dome of Melbourne Central. Above right: The pavement becomes an artist's gallery.
Below left: Southgate awaits the lunchtime cafe-crowd. Below right: More art in the street.

Melbourne: A city for shoppers

Shopping in Melbourne is a soul-satisfying experience. The city blocks offer every form of merchandising outlet known. Enjoy the suave style of Melbourne Central, with its ultra-modern, ultra-classy department store and boutiques, the more intimate venues such as Block Arcade and Royal Arcade, wide, shop-fringed thoroughfares including the tram-haunted Bourke Street Mall, and the free-for-all, everything-for-sale atmosphere of the renowned Queen Victoria Market.

★

Above: The Toorak tram is only one of Melbourne's famous fleet of trams.
Below: A Melbourne tram passes Melbourne Central.

At play in Port Phillip Bay

Port Phillip Bay provides Melbourne with a seafront which offers every recreational opportunity. You can swim, sail, or fish, watch birds, water-ski or scuba dive. Cycling and roller-blading are popular bayside activities for the young and the young-at-heart.

If it's calmer pursuits you prefer, what about strolling the St Kilda Pier, to see and be seen, after browsing in the market stalls on the Esplanade? Then sit down to coffee, or a meal, at any one of the excellent cafes and restaurants which are common in Melbourne's bayside suburbs.

✦

Above: Looking towards the city of Melbourne across Port Phillip Bay.
Below: An aerial view of Brighton.
Left: A few of the much-coveted, lovingly-maintained bathing boxes at Brighton.

51

Great Ocean Road: Harbours and headlands

The best way to explore the south-west coast of Victoria is to take the Great Ocean Road, which travels for 300 kilometres along the ocean's edge and offers access to the wonders of the Otway Ranges, as well as to other magnificent national parks.

The road was begun in 1918 and built by soldiers who had returned from the First World War to unemployment. After it had been completed in 1936, it was dedicated to those who died in the "war to end war".

Today's traveller can journey from Torquay to Anglesea to Lorne, Apollo Bay, Warrnambool and beyond, discovering relics of the whaling and timber-getting past and enjoying the superb beaches. The rainforests of the Otways offer tall timber and lovely waterfalls. To the west is Port Campbell National Park, the "Shipwreck Coast" which has claimed 142 wrecks and where the Twelve Apostles (eight to be seen from the Great Ocean Road lookouts) stand sentinel in the ocean.

———————— ✦ ————————

Above: Looking across Aireys Inlet to Fairhaven Beach, in a scenic area
accessible from Victoria's Great Ocean Road.
Opposite: East of Port Campbell stand the Twelve Apostles.

The Otway Ranges: A wildlife haven

The high rainfall of the Otway Ranges supports forests of towering mountain ash, mountain grey gum and southern blue gum, and sustains creeks and waterfalls surrounded by mossy boulders and ferns. Sheltered mountain gullies hide stands of ancient Antarctic beech trees.

Wild denizens of the Otway Ranges include around 45 species of native mammals, such as possums, kangaroos, the Platypus and the Common Wombat. There are approximately 250 species of birds, more than half of which breed in the park.

---- ★ ----

Above left: The Common Wombat spends day in a burrow, forages at night.
Above right: The Laughing Kookaburra wakes the forested ranges each dawn.
Opposite: Hopetoun Falls, one of many beautiful cascades in the Otway Ranges.

The Dandenongs: Gardens and green silences

Less than fifty kilometres from Melbourne are the Dandenong
Ranges, where magnificent forest still stands in steep-sided
gullies haunted by the voice of the lyrebird. Beautiful gardens,
galleries, restaurants, guesthouses, picnic grounds and plant
nurseries are found in abundance in the Dandenongs, but there
are still plenty of trails for the bushwalker to explore. "Puffing
Billy", a relic of the steam age, carries entranced passengers
through the ranges from Belgrave to Emerald Lake.

Healesville Sanctuary, a prime attraction of the Dandenong
area, was opened in 1934 and is noted for its remarkable
collection of Australian wildlife, including Koalas.

———————————— ✦ ————————————

Above: William Ricketts created works based on the Aboriginal concept of oneness with the environment.
Below: "Puffing Billy" chugs and toots along its track for 13 kilometres through the Dandenong Ranges.

Above: "Tilly" is just one of the charming Koalas waiting to greet visitors to Healesville Sanctuary.
Below: The Dandenongs' cool winters mean a seasonal glory of azaleas, rhododendrons and other blossoms.
Following pages: Sheep safely graze in lush pastures in a rural Victorian scene.

Rural Victoria: Life on the land

Victoria's rural areas are home to some of Australia's best-bred and most productive cattle and sheep. Its Merino wool is second to none in quality and it produces exceptionally fine dairy and beef cattle. The pastoral industry has quietly supported the State almost since the first settlement in 1834. Sheep and cattle have underwritten the boom times of the gold rushes and carried Victoria's finances through more than one lean spell. Today's pastoralists have added to their fine-woolled sheep and fat cattle a new occupation - offering old-fashioned country-style hospitality to visitors eager to experience the fascinations of life on the land.

---✦---

Opposite, top left and clockwise: Sorting the silver fleece; shearer at work; gun shearer relaxing during lunch break.
Above: Cattle ambling along a Victorian country road.

The Murray: Australia's greatest river

Water may take three months to travel the more than 2,500 kilometres from the source of the River Murray, in the Australian Alps, to the river's mouth at Lake Alexandrina. For much of its length the river forms the boundary between the States of Victoria and New South Wales and it supplies the water needs of a large number of people.

In the roaring days of the 1860s and 1870s, the Murray was a busy waterway. Echuca was home port for paddlewheelers carrying wool, timber, wheat and other cargo along the Murray. Eventually, railways took this trade away and today the paddlewheelers are treasured museum exhibits, or pleasure craft carrying happy holidaymakers.

---★---

Above: Paddlewheelers once brought wheat, timber and wool to Echuca, to be sent on by rail to Melbourne.
Right: Sunrise on the Murray River floodplains.

TASMANIA

THE WILDERNESS STATE

Tasmania does nothing by halves. When it is civilised, it echoes the gentility of an earlier age and a way of life established in Europe half a world away. When it is wild, it is wild indeed - a land of precipitous ranges, desolate high heaths, moody mountain lakes and rugged coastlines.

The island was settled by the British in 1803 and remained a penal colony for half a century. European crops, building methods and social customs transplanted easily to this temperate place. When transportation ceased in 1852, there were many solid stone constructions left to bear witness to the grim days of convict labour.

Today, Port Arthur Penal Settlement lies in ruins but Hobart, Launceston and smaller centres are a satisfying blend of new and old construction, where every street corner brings architectural discoveries and every garden is a horticultural delight.

Tasmania is a place to explore at leisure, taking time to sample some of the best seafood in the world and to appreciate the charm of hosts who have made bed-and-breakfast into an art form. There are well-made, if winding, roads which lead through pretty farming towns and fertile pastures and orchards to sheltered coves and wonderful beaches. There are other roads which lead to the magnificence of wilderness - Mount Field, Cradle Mountain and Lake St Clair, Southwest National Park, Freycinet National Park and, crowning glory for adventurers, the Franklin-Lower Gordon Wild Rivers National Park.

---✶---

Below left: An aerial view of Hobart, the capital city of Tasmania.
Below right: Secluded waters and rugged mountains ornament Tasmania's wild places.
Opposite: Victoria Dock, Hobart.
Following pages: Wrest Point Casino is to the left of this dawn vista of Hobart's Sandy Bay and the Derwent River.

Tasmania: An island full of surprises

Bass Strait is 240 kilometres wide and neither the overnight voyage on the ferry nor the briefer air trip prepares the traveller for stepping from the bustling mainland into another, more leisurely world.

There are parts of Tasmania, mainly those where logging or mineral extraction have held sway, which are less than scenic, but, wherever in the island the traveller may be, it is only a short drive to ordered farmland, or to soaring mountains, tree-hidden rivers and forests that conceal derelict huts.

Tasmania is home to some fascinating creatures. This is an island full of wildlife, from confident possums to squabbling Tasmanian Devils, inquisitive wallabies and a host of other mammals and birds. It is odds-on that the visitor to Tasmania will never see that vanished wonder the Thylacine. However, the animals readily viewed in the island's forests and swamplands, along its seashores or on its mountains, add a host of reasons to make the crossing of Bass Strait.

———————————————— ✴ ————————————————

Above: The Tasmanian Devil is a marsupial found only in the island State.
Opposite: Russell Falls, Mount Field National Park. The last Thylacine was trapped in this region in the 1930s.

Cradle Mountain-Lake St Clair National Park

An hour's drive south of the port of Devonport, Cradle Mountain-Lake St Clair National Park covers approximately 160,000 hectares and was listed by the World Heritage Committee in 1982. The 85-kilometre Overland Track connects Cradle Mountain with Lake St Clair and takes about five days to traverse. Lake St Clair, which was discovered by Europeans in 1826, has a depth of over 200 metres; it lies in a basin gouged out by two glaciers.

It is advisable to walk the Cradle Mountain-Lake St Clair track in the summer months, when it is possible to enjoy the stands of King Billy Pine, deciduous beech and Tasmanian myrtle and the mountain wildflowers with some assurance of good weather.

✶

Above: Lake Dove seen lying in front of Cradle Mountain,
in Cradle Mountain-Lake St Clair National Park.
The landscapes of the Cradle Mountain area were carved by glaciers.
Opposite: The rainforest of Cradle Mountain-Lake St Clair National Park is a world
of primeval beauty. This area is known as "the Ballroom Forest".

Tasmania's Southwest: A world heritage

The southwest of Tasmania contains country which is classed as World Heritage wilderness, almost unvisited by Europeans until recent times. Whalers harvested their living crop in the early nineteenth century; later came the timber-getters, shipping Huon Pine from Port Davey. Later still, exploration for minerals gave glimpses of the magnificence of the southwest.

The declaration of the Franklin-Lower Gordon Wild Rivers National Park in 1981 was a turning point in the story of conservation. Today, Tasmania's southwest and its southern coast are the destination of those who wish to experience some of the most beautiful and majestic of the world's remaining wild places and their remarkable plants and animals.

Above: Prion Bay and New River Lagoon. Southwest National Park.
Opposite: The rugged and sky-touched Arthur Range.

73

Richmond: Where history comes alive

The charming town of Richmond grew where travellers crossed
the Coal River 26 kilometres from Hobart, on the way to Port
Arthur. The famous Richmond Bridge is said to be haunted by
the ghost of a brutal overseer murdered by the convicts under
his command. Eventually, the Sorell Causeway stole
Richmond's traffic, allowing the town to remain a delightful
colonial relic which displays Tasmania's living history.

✳

Above: The Richmond Arms Hotel.
Below: Richmond's beautifully-kept homes add to the town's charm.
Opposite: The Richmond Bridge, Australia's oldest bridge, was built by convicts
between 1823 and 1825. Behind the bridge stands St John's Church.

Port Arthur: Relic of a grim past

Port Arthur Penal Settlement was founded in 1830 by Governor George Arthur. Inmates were expected to undertake "the most unceasing labour" under "the most harassing vigilance". They worked from dawn until nightfall in silence. When the gaol was closed in 1877, the buildings were abandoned. Some have now been restored by the National Parks and Wildlife Service. The horrors of the past are easy to imagine when wandering amongst the ruins, looking at the Model Prison, where solitary confinement and "soundless, sightless isolation" replaced the lash, or reflecting on the Isle of the Dead, where nearly 1,800 convicts and 200 officials and free settlers were buried.

———————✸———————

Opposite: Ruined chapel, Port Arthur Penal Settlement.
Above: Port Arthur's prison walls have been breached by fire and time.

SOUTH AUSTRALIA

THE FESTIVAL STATE

South Australia originated as a colony of free settlers. However, the stately buildings of Adelaide are at no disadvantage compared to edifices constructed by convict labour in other State capitals. Surveyor-General Colonel William Light's design was magnificently realised and today the green city of Adelaide, sheltered by pleasant hills and near to the waters of St Vincent Gulf, is a wonderful place to explore at leisure.

A short stroll along North Terrace reveals many fascinating buildings - Government House, the War Memorial, the State Library, Museum, the Art Gallery, Adelaide University, the Railway Station and the Casino, and a host of monuments. A few steps more bring to view the stunning Adelaide Festival Centre, with its concert hall and theatres. A street away is the shopper's paradise, Rundle Mall and the sightseer can then walk on to admire majestic Victoria Square.

Near to Adelaide, in the Mount Lofty Ranges and in the Barossa Valley, German settlers pioneered fertile areas, where today picturesque towns such as Hahndorf and Tanunda are famous for old-world hospitality, vineyards and a flourish of festivals. McLaren Vale is another notable winemaking area south of Adelaide. The beautiful beaches of the Fleurieu Peninsula and the seaside resort of Victor Harbor are well worth a visit, while a ferry from Cape Jervis makes the short voyage to Kangaroo Island, which offers scenic national parks and wildlife.

The rugged Flinders Ranges, with their changing colours and stark beauty, lie north of Adelaide. The Yorke Peninsula is a water-sports playground and the Eyre Peninsula offers superb beaches and stunning coastal scenery. Inland are opal towns such as Coober Pedy, while legendary Lake Eyre awaits the adventurer. The State's southeast is a triangle of lakes, forests and farms, fertile and green by courtesy of the River Murray, which flows to the sea near the wilderness of the Coorong, with its wealth of bird life.

Below: Adelaide's biennial Festival of the Arts is internationally famous.
Opposite: Twilight over Torrens Lake, a scenic feature of Adelaide created by impeding the flow of the River Torrens.
Following pages: An aerial view of Adelaide, with Torrens Lake and the Festival Centre in the foreground.

Adelaide: A city for discoveries

No visit to Adelaide is complete without a journey in the famous Bay Tram from Victoria Square to the top of Jetty Road. Once, Glenelg was a seaside resort for the well-to-do, now it is everyone's playground. Other Adelaide entertainments include visiting the Casino, eating at any of an enormous range of restaurants, going to the Central Market, or searching out art and crafts at galleries and workshops.

Above left and right: The Victoria Square Fountain; aerial view of Glenelg, where early settlers came ashore on the mainland. Below left and right: Adelaide Casino and Railway Station on North Terrace; sidewalk cafes at Glenelg.

South Australia: The Festival State

The internationally-renowned Adelaide Festival of Arts is held for three weeks in March every second year, while the Come Out Youth Festival takes place in the year between. Glendi is the Southern Hemisphere's largest Greek festival.

There are Vintage Festivals in the Barossa and the wineries of the Fleurieu Peninsula. The Barossa wineries also host an annual Gourmet Weekend. McLaren Vale holds a Bushing Festival in October, Willunga holds a Springtime Almond Blossom Festival, while in January Hahndorf holds its famous German Schutzenfest. The Riverland has its own festivals and oceanside Port Lincoln holds a Tunarama Festival.

✦

Above: The Adelaide Festival Centre is a focus for artistic activity.

The Barossa: A valley of vineyards

In 1837, Colonel Light, a veteran of the Napoleonic Wars, named an area north of Adelaide "barrosa", or "hill of roses", after a battle in the Spanish Peninsula, which coincidentally took place in a wine-making area. The present-day Barossa Valley is about 30 kilometres long and its fertile soil, hot, dry summers and reliable winter rains are well-suited to the cultivation of wine-making grapes. There are more than 30 Lutheran churches in the valley and their spires, rising about the trim and tidy valley towns, reflect the area's German and strongly religious heritage.

Above: An historic store in the town of Tanunda.
Below: One of the Barossa Valley's many craft shops.
Right: Tanunda is known as "the gateway to the Barossa".
Following pages: Flinders Ranges National Park.

The Flinders Ranges: Scenic and popular

The scenic Flinders Ranges, approximately 430 kilometres north of Adelaide, are popular for touring, walking, climbing and camping. The Flinders Ranges National Park extends over nearly 100,000 hectares of the ecologically fragile ranges.

★

Above: A Wallaroo thuds away amongst summertime Flinders Ranges vegetation.
Centre: The Flinders Ranges rise abruptly from the plain.
Below: Spectacular Wilpena Pound reaches 1,200 metres in height at St Mary's Peak.
Opposite: Sturt's Desert Pea, floral emblem of South Australia, is common in the Flinders Ranges.

Playing Outback

South Australia has a population of 1.5 million, is rich in mineral wealth and is one of Australia's most industrialised States. Most of the primary industries, such as fishing and the cultivation of vines and orchards, are coastal. The people of the Outback make a living from sheep, cattle or mining. They exist in a tough landscape and work hard, and when they get together to play they thoroughly enjoy themselves.

Above: Australian Football rules in South Australia!
Opposite: The William Creek Gymkhana raises funds for the Flying Doctor Service.

Kangaroo Island: Beauty and wildlife

Kangaroo Island, half an hour's flight from Adelaide (or catch the ferry from Cape Jervis to Penneshaw), is Australia's third-largest island and contains sixteen national and conservation parks. Sealers and whalers had worked the area for three decades before the first official British settlers landed in 1836. Today, the island's wildlife is a bonus added to scenic attractions.

✳

Above: The lighthouse at Cape de Couedic was built in 1906. A flying-fox was used to haul materials up the cliff from the sea to the site.
Below: At Seal Bay Conservation Park, several hundred Australian Sea-lions form a breeding colony.
Opposite: The Remarkable Rocks are large, angular, weathered granite blocks, standing on the granite dome of Kirkpatrick Point.

The Eyre Peninsula: Seafood and spectacular scenery

Port Lincoln, on the south-east of the tip of the Eyre Peninsula, is famous for its fishing fleet and seafood and is an ideal base for expeditions to view some very beautiful coastal country. Coffin Bay National Park, 50 kilometres east of Port Lincoln, offers dunes, headlands and lovely bays, as well as plenty of wildlife. Kellidie Bay Conservation Park is an extension of Coffin Bay National Park. Lincoln National Park, with its coastline of precipitous cliffs, is only 25 kilometres south of Port Lincoln.

———————————— ✸ ————————————

Above: Coffin Bay National Park, on the southern extremity of the Eyre Peninsula.
Opposite: Cape Carnot lies southwest of Port Lincoln.

WESTERN AUSTRALIA

THE WILDFLOWER STATE

The twin cities of Perth, capital of Western Australia and historic Fremantle, its port, are linked by the Swan River, which meanders from the Darling scarp, then flows under the Causeway and widens into Perth Water. The river squeezes itself under the Narrows Bridge, is joined by the Canning River, spreads out into Melville Water and finally reaches the sea between the man-made North and South Moles at Fremantle.

The banks of the Swan are lined with gracious homes, sailboat clubs and parks where many come to picnic and play in, or beside, the water. Those who do not care for these delights can drive to the Indian Ocean, which offers a smorgasbord of easily-accessible beaches.

To discover vast Western Australia, begin the journey in June, in the far northern Kimberley region. Here are fantastic ranges, craggy gorges and wide golden plains scattered with Boab trees and termite mounds. July could be spent in the scenic Pilbara and at Ningaloo National Park and exploring Shark Bay, with its friendly dolphins. Then move south in August, to sample seafood and the easy life in Carnarvon and Geraldton, then visit Kalbarri and Nambung National Parks and see the coastal heaths ablaze with wildflowers.

September and October should be spent in the southwest, sampling the wines of the Swan Valley, exploring Perth and Fremantle, then touring south past Bunbury and Busselton to Cape Naturaliste and Cape Leeuwin. Then, as the weather warms and the wildflowers spread their glory into cooler places, move to the south coast and its wonderful National Parks - the Stirling Ranges, Fitzgerald River, Cape Le Grand and Cape Arid. (You can save the fascinating Goldfields for next winter.)

It's Australia's largest State and if you've never been there, start planning a visit now!

★

Below: The Black Swan, seen here with cygnets, is the faunal emblem of the State of Western Australia.
Opposite: The Pinnacles are limestone pillars rising from the coastal sands of Nambung National Park.

Above left: Weekend barbecue in the parklands bordering the Swan River.
Above right: A number of yacht clubs provide excellent facilities on the Swan River.
Below left: An aerial view of Fremantle shows Elder Place in foreground, Fremantle oval top left,
and the Fishing Boat Harbour and Success Harbour top right.
Below right: Sunworshippers on one of Perth's magnificent beaches.
Opposite: An aerial view across Perth city from Northbridge towards the Darling Range.
Following pages: A night view of Perth from Kings Park.

Above: The limestone headlands of Rottnest Island shelter wonderful clearwater coves.
Below: Thomson Bay settlement viewed over the Rottnest Lighthouse and (right) Pinky Beach.

Rottnest Island: Where Quokkas roam free

Rottnest Island is 20 kilometres northwest of Fremantle. It is eleven kilometres by five, with a coastline full of delightful bays and beaches. Sensible development has kept much of the island's charm unspoiled - no private cars are allowed - and Dutch Captain Willem de Vlamingh's 1696 description of Rottnest as "terrestrial paradise" seems still suitable three centuries later. Vlamingh thought the little hopping animals he saw on the island were rats (hence the name "rats' nest"). They are Quokkas, marsupials related to wallabies, which today amicably share their island with delighted holidaymakers.

✦

Above: The Quokka, a small marsupial related to the wallabies, is very common on Rottnest but not often seen on the mainland.

Floral beauty

The flora of Western Australia is world-renowned amongst botanists because of the large number of unique plant species included. To non-scientists, the West's wildflowers are simply staggering in variety of shape and colour.

✦

Above left and clockwise: Yellow Buttercup; Fringed Lily; Morning Iris; Scarlet Banksia.

The flowering Southwest

The sandplains and heaths on both sides of Australia support a great variety of flowering plants. In Western Australia, these areas extend from Perth north almost to Shark Bay and along the South Coast as far east as Cape Arid.

★

Above left and clockwise: Mangles Kangaroo Paw; Orange Banksia; Baxter's Kunzea; Everlasting Daisies.

The Southwest: Fertile and friendly

Southwest Western Australia has some of the continent's greenest pastures, mightiest trees and most dramatic coastline. Albany, the first town established in the State, is one of many centres for farming and pastoral activities, and stands near some of Australia's most dramatic coastal scenery.

★

Above left and right: Wave Rock, near Hyden, is a spectacular granite formation; surfer near Albany.
Below left and right: The towered Albany Post Office; herding sheep is a family activity on this southwest farm.

Southwestern wilderness: Nature's kingdom

The coasts of southwest and southern Western Australia deserve a leisurely visit if the traveller is to appreciate the full beauty of wave-pounded, rocky headlands and beautiful bays and beaches. Inland, are tall forests and bird-rich heathland, which is ablaze with wildflowers in Spring.

Above left and right: Granite boulders are typical of the southern coast of Western Australia; Fitzgerald River National Park.
Below left and right: Two Peoples Bay near Albany; the Stirling Ranges, famous for wildflowers, consist of rounded, gravelly mountains.

Above left and right: The jasper outcrop which gives the nearby town of Marble Bar its name; the Hamersley Range.
Below left and right: Ancient folded rock strata are characteristic of the Pilbara; Weano Gorge, in the Hamersley Range.

The Pilbara: An iron land

The ancient rocks of the Pilbara originated more than 2,500 million years ago as sediments of iron and silica deposited on the floor of an ancient ocean. Today, the massive iron ore deposits of the area generate mining, whose support towns form handy bases for exploring the area. In the Pilbara, red, eroded ranges are dotted with spinifex grasses and pale-trunked eucalypts, while coolibahs and cajeputs grow along dry watercourses. The Hamersley Range National Park, also known as Karijini National Park, covers 600,000 hectares and offers spectacular ranges, whose deep gorges conceal pools which attract birds and other wildlife.

✦

Above: The ancient rock mass which forms the northwest corner of Australia was long ago lifted high above sea level, folded and buckled, then dissected into deep gorges by rivers and eroded by eons of weathering.

The Kimberley: Cattle country

Between 1883 and 1886, cattle were driven overland to the Kimberley from the Eastern States. Today, in many areas of the Kimberley, mobs of station cattle still roam unimpeded by fences. Sometimes as feral as the donkeys and pigs which co-exist in the area, they are mustered in the Dry season by stockmen whose skills equal any attributed to the legendary cowboys of the Old West. A ringer can stay on anything with a mane and tail, but today the thunder of hooves may be accompanied by the chatter of helicopter blades where beasts have to be retrieved from particularly tough country.

✦

Left: The Boab tree grows on sandy plains, on stony hillsides and beside creeks and billabongs in the west and east of the Kimberley.
Above and below: Today's stockmen still begin work before dawn and finish after sunset.

Above: A rugged Kimberley landscape.
*Below: Prince Regent River National Park, one of the world's
remaining wilderness areas.*

Above: Purnululu (Bungle Bungle) National Park was established in 1987.
The domes rise to 300 metres above the plain and are made of easily-eroded sandstone.
Below: The Fitzroy River flows for over 600 kilometres from the Durack Range to King Sound near the town of Derby.

NORTHERN TERRITORY

AUSTRALIA'S TOP END

Port Darwin was named after naturalist Charles Darwin in 1839. The town of Palmerston was established there in 1869; its name was officially changed to Darwin by the Federal Government in 1911.

The bombing of Darwin during World War Two and the destruction caused by Cyclone Tracy in 1974 left their impact, in military relics and memorials, and a rebuilt, cyclone-resistant city. Today's Darwin, which is geographically closer to Asia than to other Australian capitals, is a multicultural modern city. A sojourn in Darwin should include a tour of the excellent Museum of Arts and Sciences and the East Point War Museum. Other attractions include the magnificent Botanic Gardens, Darwin Mall, the Diamond Beach Casino and the markets at Mindil Beach. Within an easy drive from the city are Howard Springs Nature Reserve, bird-rich Fogg Dam Conservation Reserve, the South Alligator River with its famous Saltwater Crocodiles and the excellent Territory Wildlife Park.

The Top End in the summer monsoon season can be hot and very wet, but there are good all-weather roads from Darwin to Litchfield National Park, with its wonderful waterfalls, and to Kakadu National Park, where rain falling on the stone escarpment floods the coastal wetlands. In the Wet, some attractions are almost inaccessible. However, the surging vitality of the Top End at this time is memorable. In the Dry season, it is possible to penetrate the country more deeply, see birds and other wildlife concentrated on billabongs and waterways and travel in comfort in the pleasant winter sunshine. A visit to Katherine Gorge (Nitmiluk National Park), three hours' drive from Darwin along the Stuart Highway, will give one last memorable experience of calm waters reflecting towering sandstone cliffs, before travelling southwards towards the Red Centre.

Above: Black citizens and white citizens of the Territory have much to learn from each other.
Opposite: An aerial view of Darwin city.

Top End wetlands: Birdwatchers' paradise

During the Dry season, waterbirds congregate around rivercourses and billabongs across the Top End and are easily viewed. As the floodplains fill after the Wet breaks, the birds spread out to feed and to nest. Access for birdwatchers is more difficult, but the insights into breeding behaviour to be gained are fascinating.

---- ✸ ----

Above: Birdwatchers on Yellow Water, Kakadu National Park.
Below: Kakadu wetlands provide ideal breeding grounds for waterbirds, crocodiles, fish, frogs and insects.
Opposite top to bottom: Magpie Geese; Whistling-ducks; Egrets.

Kakadu: Ramparts of stone

The sandstone escarpment that forms the edge of the ancient Arnhem Land Plateau stretches for 600 kilometres across the Top End. Massive outliers isolated by erosion from the plateau stand on the plain, refuges for wallabies and rock-loving birds. Aboriginal art in caves and overhangs of the "stone country" provides a record dating back tens of thousands of years. In the Wet season, rain falls in torrents on the escarpment, drops over the edge in spectacular waterfalls, then floods into the rivers and wetlands of the coastal plains below.

Above left and right: Aboriginal art at Nourlangie Rock, Kakadu National Park; Ubirr, Kakadu National Park.
Below left and right: Stone country, Ubirr, Kakadu National Park; Aboriginal art is common in caves and overhangs in Kakadu.
Opposite: Twin Falls, seen here in the Wet season, is a spectacular feature of Kakadu National Park.

THE RED CENTRE

AUSTRALIA'S LIVING HEART

The most remote area of Australia, right in the centre of this enormous continent, is also the easiest for which to map out a sightseeing itinerary. Fly or drive south from Darwin, north from Adelaide or west from Brisbane to Alice Springs, then set out on the grand tour of the famous sights of The Centre.

This desert country is safe for those who obey the rules. Either travel with a reputable public carrier, or make sure your vehicle is in good order, carry water and stay on main roads.

Near to Alice are the MacDonnell Ranges, with their gaps and gorges: Ormiston Gorge and Pound, N'Dhala Gorge and Trephina Gorge. Further afield are Finke Gorge National Park, with its primeval Palm Valley, the fantastic red gorge of Watarrka (Kings Canyon) and statuesque, solitary Itirkawara (Chambers Pillar).

The Lasseter Highway will lead to Australia's best-known monuments, magnificent Uluru (Ayers Rock) and many-headed Kata Tjuta (the Olgas). Uluru rises 348 metres above the plain and is the eroded top of an enormous underground sandstone mountain. Kata Tjuta is a group of smooth domes. Like other less massive formations in this light-haunted country, they change colours as the sun crosses the sky and afford striking views at sunrise and sunset.

Apart from sun-resistant birds and insects, wildlife in these regions can be elusive unless the watcher is prepared to walk at dawn or dusk. In these cooler hours, desert-wise animals forage, while those which need to drink come to water hidden in the clefts of the ranges.

✶

Below: Alice Springs is located almost in the middle of Australia and is an ideal base from which to explore the MacDonnell Ranges and other scenic features of the Centre. Opposite: Itirkawara (Chambers Pillar) is a sandstone remnant of a long-eroded range of hills.

121

The Simpson Desert: A living heart

The plants of the Red Centre are well-adapted to long periods without rain. Their leaves are reduced in size, or covered with hairs or wax, to prevent excess water-loss; some, like saltbush and bluebush, can excrete the salt their roots draw from the soil. In a dry spell - which may last for years - the red sand and blue sky dominate the subdued silvery grey-greens and browns of the vegetation. After rain, hidden seeds sprout and shoot, and old stems put out new leaves. The desert plants blossom in a multitude of colours. This vegetable wealth, new-set seeds and multiplying insects provide a rich feast for birds and small mammals and for a brief time the desert is a garden of plenty.

✴

Above: The Simpson Desert after rain. Desert plants blossom after rain and set seed which will endure through the next dry spell.
Opposite: In the arid north-east of South Australia, desert plants grow where their roots reach water, but sand-dunes stand bare.

The MacDonnells: Rugged red ranges

The MacDonnell Ranges stretch in east-to-west ridges across Central Australia. Ancient river systems once flowed north to south across them, cutting great gorges through the hard Heavitree Quartz which is a major constituent of the ranges. Standley Chasm, Simpsons Gap, Ormiston Gorge, Haasts Bluff, Trephina Gorge and Arltunga Historical Reserve are all places to discover in the MacDonnells.

✦

Above: The MacDonnell Ranges run in a series of ridges across the centre of Australia.
Opposite: Cool water in Ormiston Gorge and Pound National Park, in the Western MacDonnell Ranges.

Above: The Wild Horse Race at the annual Alice Springs Rodeo, a major Territory event.
Below: Moving a mob of cattle along on the Barkly Tablelands.
Opposite: A competitor in the Bending Race at the Alice Springs Rodeo.

Uluṟu: The monolith

Uluṟu National Park is in the southwest corner of the Territory, 460 kilometres from Alice Springs. It is easy to make the pilgrimage by air, but many prefer to approach Uluṟu after crossing the vastness of the desert. If, during some cooler moment in the five hours' drive, they take the time to stop and explore a little on foot, they will discover that this arid land is home to fascinating plants and animals.

No photograph and no words can prepare the newcomer for the vastness and majesty of the Rock, or the effects of sunlight and shadow upon its surfaces. Two groups of Aboriginal people, the Yankunytjatjara and the Pitjantjatjara, belong to the area, which for them has special significance. Restrictions placed upon visitors by these traditional owners and by the Australian Nature Conservation Agency should be respected.

———————————— ✸ ————————————

Above: Uluṟu the tip of a buried mountain.
Opposite top to bottom: Waiting to watch the sunset light on Uluṟu;
climbing Uluṟu; a guide interprets Uluṟu to visitors.

Kata Tjuta: "Memorials from ancient times"

Kata Tjuta is 32 kilometres from Uluru and Mount Olga, the highest of Kata Tjuta's many domes, rises 200 metres above the highest point of the Rock. There are more than 30 great dome-shaped boulders, covering an area of about 30 square kilometres in all. Between the individual domes are narrow ravines, many of which contain rock pools in their shaded depths.

Visitors to Kata Tjuta and Uluru can make their base at Yulara International Tourist Resort, a "low-impact oasis" built outside the boundary of Uluru National Park and opened in 1984.

Above: Kata Tjuta means "many heads".
Below: Kata Tjuta was described by Ernest Giles in 1872 as "rounded minarets, giant cupolas and monstrous domes ... memorials from the ancient times of earth".

Above: In the Centre, the Red Kangaroo lives where native grasses and water are available.
Below: The Bilby is a rare bandicoot, which shelters from the daytime heat in a burrow.

Above: The Wedgetailed Eagle soars high above the arid land. It may be seen at closer quarters feeding on road kills.
Below: The Dingo, Australia's wild dog, does not bark but howls. It may hunt over a wide area, but needs access to water.

QUEENSLAND

THE SUNSHINE STATE

Queensland's capital city, Brisbane, is in the extreme south-east of a big State with many rich natural resources. There is plenty of room for a number of regional centres of population to flourish where Nature's semitropical and tropical gifts are especially bountiful.

Toowoomba, queen city of the fertile Darling Downs, is less than two hours' drive west from Brisbane, while, to the south and north of the capital, are the Gold Coast and the Sunshine Coast. Northwards lie coastal cities like Rockhampton, the beef capital of Australia, with its wonderful colonial homes, Townsville, the north's administrative centre with its world-famous marine research facilities, and Cairns, a tropical and cosmopolitan city which is the gateway to the Far North, especially for international visitors.

Take a long, leisurely journey of exploration, from the Gold Coast right up to the wilderness of Cape York. Explore the coastal rainforest, play in the Whitsunday Islands and enjoy the Great Barrier Reef. On the return trip, detour inland past magnificent outlying spurs of the Great Divide, through some of Australia's best grazing land and experience the Outback celebrated in the Stockman's Hall of Fame at Longreach.

Brisbane itself is Australia's friendliest city, where outdoor living has been elevated into an art form. Set on its lazy river, Brisbane can equal the sophistication of southern capitals, while adding its own laid-back lifestyle. South Bank and Riverside, the magnificent Performing Arts Complex, Queen Street Mall, theatres, shops, boutiques and wonderful restaurants - Brisbane offers these, plus tropical gardens and a garland of surrounding forests and national parks.

———————————✹———————————

Below: Sailing in the Whitsunday Islands.
Opposite: Whitehaven Beach, Whitsunday Island.

Brisbane: A sociable city

Since the 1988 World Expo showed the way, Brisbane has taken many giant leaps forward in the areas of hospitality and entertainment. South Bank now stands on the Expo site, near the State Library, the Art Gallery, Performing Arts Complex and Museum. The Brisbane River, slipping under its four great city bridges, bordered by jacaranda and poinciana trees, is a quiet background to these and many other city landmarks.

Brisbane was a penal settlement from 1824 until 1839. In the late nineteenth century it became a busy port, in the twentieth a centre of industry and commerce. As the twenty-first century dawns, Brisbane is a fast-growing, prosperous city. Homes in inner suburbs are highly prized and lovingly restored by their happy owners and the Brisbane lifestyle makes the most of southeast Queensland's warm, sunny climate.

Above: South Bank stands beside the Brisbane River on the site of World Expo 88.
Below: Paddington, one of Brisbane's older suburbs.
Left: The lights of Brisbane, capital of Queensland, reflected in the Brisbane River.

137

The Gold Coast: Sunblessed sands

The 43 kilometres of beach which form Queensland's Gold Coast bask in sunshine around three hundred days of each year. The Coast is cooled by the blue-green Pacific Ocean and can offer a lifestyle as simple or as worldly as the heart desires. Sea World and Warner Brothers Movie World attract many, while others prefer to browse in modern shopping centres, or just lie on the beach. At Currumbin Sanctuary, wild lorikeets come to be fed.

A short distance inland is a world of ancient rainforests, waterfalls and unique wildlife. The parks in and near the MacPherson Ranges, including Lamington, Mt Cougal, Springbrook and Mt Tamborine, are full of wild places of heart-stopping beauty, whose cool green shade contrasts with and complements the golden, sun-warmed beaches of the Coast.

———————— ★ ————————

Above: Warm sun, cool sand, blue sky and sparkling sea are everlasting attractions at the Gold Coast.
Below: The surf is up, the sun is shining - who could ask for more?
Left: The highrise buildings of Surfers Paradise stand between the Pacific Ocean and the Nerang River.

The Sunshine Coast: A secret shared

Until recent years, the Sunshine Coast just north of Brisbane was less well-known than its southern rival and those who prized its peace and magnificent beaches were not unhappy to have it so. Today, the secret is out. The attractions of the area, which include the coastal holiday towns of Caloundra, Noosa and Maroochydore, scenic Bribie Island and Coolum Beach, and extends northwards to the magnificent Cooloola National Park, are widely appreciated.

The hinterland encompasses fertile farmlands and dramatic mountain scenery, including the volcanic remnants which, in 1770, Captain James Cook named the Glasshouse Mountains. National Parks to be explored here offer forested ranges and also coastal plains typical of the original heathland of the area, rich in flowering plants and in birds and mammals.

---✷---

Above: The Glasshouse Mountains, just north of Brisbane, were once volcanic vents.
Opposite: At anchor in Pumicestone Passage, between Bribie Island and mainland Queensland.

The Birdsville Hotel: The loneliest pub

Birdsville, at the northern end of the Birdsville Track, has been a famous watering-place on the Queensland-South Australia stock route since the 1870s. The town stands in Queensland, just north of the South Australian border and just west of the red sand-dunes of the Simpson Desert.

In August-September each year, the famous Birdsville Hotel serves up to 5,000 people during the Birdsville Races, which were first held in 1882. Today, funds from this popular event go to the Royal Flying Doctor Service.

★

Left: The Birdsville Hotel is an oasis in the arid Outback.
Above: After rain falls, flowers decorate the dunes of the Simpson Desert.

Lawn Hill: A jewel in Queensland's crown

Lawn Hill National Park is near the Queensland-Northern Territory border and can be reached by driving south of Burketown and taking the track west from Gregory Downs bush pub. The Park was opened in 1985 and covers 12,000 hectares.

That much can be learned from the map. What cannot be conveyed by any map is the surprise and delight the traveller feels after crossing the arid plains to find Lawn Hill's sandstone gorge, with walls up to 70 metres in height. Its cool, clear creeks and waterfalls are surrounded by lush tropical vegetation, including pandanus, figs, cajeputs and Livistona palms. No wonder it is known as "the jewel in the crown of Queensland's National Parks".

✴

Above: Canoeing through paradise - in Lawn Hill Gorge.
Right: Lawn Hill Gorge.

What is a Queenslander?

The term "Queenslander" may mean a person or a style of architecture. The typical wooden "Queenslander" stands on stilts, which provides extra living space below the house, has wide verandahs, high ceilings and a steep iron roof, which quickly sheds tropical downpours and allows possums to occupy their own attic space. All is directed to providing shade and to allowing air to circulate freely. The "Queenslander" is usually surrounded by a garden of lush tropical vegetation.

A journey north through coastal towns will provide a visual feast of "Queenslanders" and will provide views of other Queenslanders at their daily occupations, one of the most picturesque of which is cane-farming. Other Queenslanders up here run cattle, go fishing, extract minerals or, increasingly, are involved in welcoming visitors to the exciting tropical North.

✦

Above and below: Cooktown's architecture is a blend of the practical and the elegant. The funds for the latter can often be traced to the gold rushes of the 1870s. This Rockhampton "Queenslander" stands on stilts, has wide verandahs and breezeways.
Opposite above and below: Cairns, chief city of tropical Northern Queensland; sugar cane is a staple crop in Queensland's coastal north.

Toowoomba: A flowering city

Toowoomba stands on the edge of the Great Divide and the highway from Brisbane winds steeply up "the Range" before emerging into a town of gracious gardens and pleasant parks. This centre for the prosperous Darling Downs holds four annual celebrations: Green Week is in April, Gardenfest in May, the Carnival of Flowers and Farmfest in September. The area's first European settlers were pastoralists, but by the early twentieth century the success of mixed farming in the area brought grain silos, butter, cheese and bacon factories to the towns of the Darling Downs.

✦

Above: Sunset over Toowoomba, the major centre of the fertile Darling Downs.

Queensland's Outback: "G'day mate!"

Outback Queensland boasts multitudes of sheep and cattle and some of the friendliest, most hospitable humans on the face of the earth. Winton, Longreach, Blackall, Barcaldine - these are towns where someone is always ready to stop and yarn about floods, fires, droughts, mouse and grasshopper plagues and the good times which went between all the disasters. This is the home of Qantas Airlines and the Australian Labor Party and of a dream which became ironclad reality, the Stockman's Hall of Fame, which owes its origins to the vision of the legendary RM Williams and the noted bush artist Hugh Sawrey.

Above: The Stockman's Hall of Fame in Longreach is a monument to the people of Australia's Outback.

Overland!

There are plenty of stories associated with Queensland's cattle country. In 1870, Harry Redford (Captain Starlight) and four mates "acquired" around 1,000 beasts at Longreach and drove them nearly 2,500 kilometres over uncharted country to South Australia. The cattle were sold, but Redford was arrested, sent back to Queensland and tried at Roma. The jury, quite properly admiring his feat, returned a verdict of Not Guilty and Rolf Boldrewood immortalised the tale in *Robbery Under Arms*.

---✦---

Above: Cattle of tropical breeds have proved ideal for the warmer parts of Queensland.
Opposite: Youngsters grow up fast in the remote areas of the Outback.

The Great Barrier Reef: It's magic!

The stretch of warm clear tropic sea and coral we call the Great Barrier Reef contains nearly three thousand individual reefs and about four hundred islands. Composed of four hundred or more kinds of soft and hard corals, it stretches from Papua New Guinea to the Bunker Group, east of Bundaberg, on Queensland's continental shelf. The Reef was recognised as a World Heritage area in 1981. It is, quite simply, one of the wonders of the world and to visit it and experience what it has to offer is one of the wonders of anyone's lifetime.

———————✦———————

Above: A coral reef is home to myriads of fish and other marine animals.
Below: Gorgonian coral and diver.
Opposite: Lady Musgrave, one of the islands scattered like jewels across Great Barrier Reef waters.

Fraser: The great sand island

Fraser Island is 123 kilometres long, averages 14 kilometres wide and is about 184,000 hectares in area. At Fraser it is possible to fish, swim in the sea or in one of the island's beautiful freshwater lakes, explore primeval rainforests, or admire stunning cliffs of eight-million-year-old coloured sands, and sand-dunes which may reach 230 metres in height. This largest sand island in the world is a Heritage area, the first site listed on the register of Australia's National Estate.

Above: Fishing is popular and productive on the islands of the Great Sandy Region.
Left: A Dingo explores a Fraser Island beach.

The rainforest: A living cathedral

To walk in rainforest is to step into a living cathedral. Far above, the vaulted roof is a canopy of leaves, where pigeons and parrots chorus as they search for bright fruits. Tall trunks descend like pillars from the leaves and prop themselves on the damp soil with winged buttress roots. They are linked by creepers, ornamented with orchids and ferns and their bark is bright as stained-glass with lichens and mosses. From somewhere deeper in the forest comes the muted summons of a waterfall, beckoning you deeper into this majestic green world.

✸

Above: The King Parrot is a brilliant inhabitant of the rainforest.
Opposite: Chalahn Falls, in Lamington National Park, Queensland.

Discover Australia!

The best way to discover Australia is to travel around its wide expanses, taking your time, appreciating its landscapes, wildlife and people. You don't need to mount a major expedition, which will take six months to complete and cover thousands of kilometres. Explore areas close to home at first, then extend your operations further afield.

Before you set out, it is a good idea to learn something about the Australia you will discover. There is plenty of information available on Australia's many National Parks, its wildlife and its cities and towns.

Generally, it is wise to visit northern and central Australia in the Dry season, from May to October, when the weather is comparatively cool and dry. Southern Australia, including Tasmania and the East coast, offers great experiences year-round, though winter in more southerly areas may be chilly. South-west Western Australia with its wildflowers is particularly attractive in Spring and the Great Barrier Reef is magic at any time.

Rushing from place to place, one eye on a timetable, is not the best way to discover this great land. If you can do so, take your time and regard the journey as being as important as the destination. Early morning and late afternoon are the best times to view landscapes and wildlife. Remember that special permits may be necessary to camp in some areas and to visit Aboriginal land. Wherever you go in the Outback treat the land and its inhabitants with respect - leave no souvenirs of your visit and take away only photographs and memories.

Every now and then on your journey, climb from your transport, walk away, then stop, look and listen. Take a deep breath and savour the scents of the land. Look near and far. Feel the texture of trees and rocks, water and sand against your skin.

Discover Australia with all your senses and make it part of your heart and soul.

★

The map shows the location of some of Australia's national parks and reserves. Their names are listed below.

Blue Mountains 1	Cradle Mountain-Lake St Clair.....................10	Flinders Chase 19
Kosciuszko...2	Franklin-Lower Gordon Wild Rivers............11	Seal Bay...20
Bogong...3	Southwest 12	Cape Arid 21
Wilsons Promontory.......................................4	Mount Field 13	Cape Le Grand..22
Otway...5	Tasman Peninsula 14	Fitzgerald River...23
Port Campbell...6	Coffin Bay 15	Stirling Ranges...24
Grampians..7	Lincoln 16	Two People Bay-Mt Manypeaks.....................25
Ben Lomond 8	Coorong 17	Leeuwin-Naturaliste 26
Freycinet..9	Flinders Ranges 18	Nambung...27

Kalbarri 28
Cape Range 29
Karijini (Hamersley Range) 30
Purnululu (Bungle Bungle) 31
Tunnel Creek.......................................32
Windjana Gorge...................................33
Kakadu...34
Nitmiluk (Katherine Gorge) 35
Litchfield..36

Finke Gorge..37
Ormiston Gorge and Pound.....................38
Watarrka (Kings Canyon) 39
Uluru...40
Lawn Hill 41
Iron Range 42
Cape Tribulation 43
Daintree...44
Palmerston 45

Whitsunday Islands....................................46
Porcupine Gorge 47
Carnarvon 48
Great Sandy 49
Bunya Mountains 50
Cooloola...51
Lamington 52
Barrington Tops.......................................53
Warrumbungle...54

It's impossible alone

Many people have contributed directly and indirectly to the creation and publication of this book. I would like to thank you all sincerely.

To acquire some of the images, co-operation was required from several departments of Australia's National Parks and Wildlife Services. Particular thanks are due to the Federal, South Australian and Queensland Departments. Special thanks also to Phillip Hayson, for his great photograph of Sydney Opera House lit for the triumphant Olympic Games 2000 announcement.

The majority of the photographs were exposed with Nikon 35mm F4 cameras and some with a Mamiya 120mm RBZ camera. The film used ranged from Kodachrome 64ASA to Ektachrome X and Ektachrome EPZ 64ASA and 100ASA, the latter processed by Prolab of Queensland.

Finally, but never last in my thoughts, I would like to thank Jan Parish and the national sales and administrative staff of Steve Parish Publishing Pty Ltd. My wife and partner, Jan has accompanied me on many expeditions - thank you Jan, for everything you are and everything you have done for me and for Steve Parish Publishing.

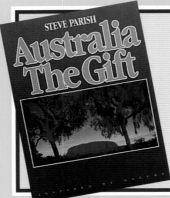

Australia The Gift
A COMPANION BOOK

Australia The Gift contains images selected by Steve Parish from hundreds of thousands of photographs he has taken all over Australia. The words which accompany these superb pictures offer rare insight into the perceptions and emotions of a man who has made recording Australia on film and in words his lifetime passion. **Australia the Gift** is a joyous celebration of a unique continent in all its variety.

AVAILABLE THROUGH ALL GOOD BOOKSTORES AND STEVE PARISH STOCKISTS

First published in Australia, 1994, Steve Parish Publishing Pty Ltd
PO Box 1058 Archerfield BC Queensland 4108
© copyright Steve Parish Publishing Pty Ltd, 1994
Reprinted 1996 (twice)
Reprinted 1997, 1999
Printed in Hong Kong
ISBN 0 947263 74 8

PRODUCTION DETAILS
Photography - Steve Parish
Text - Pat Slater
Design - Paul Byrne
Computer artwork - Phillipa McConnel - Oats